ISBN 978-1-300-69355-0
www.marydalton.co.uk

Foreword

This book is to celebrate not just food, but printmaking. This paperback text is a version of an original limited edition illustrated book hand typeset by The Whittington Press and printed by myself at the Washroom Press. As a master printmaker I am passionate about this unique art form and keen to support all those who believe in its expression. Having collaborated with some of the UK's finest artists in print studios, I have always found a link between printmaking and food. Odd as it sounds, nearly all of the wonderful print masters I have learned from have a keen interest in food, be it bread making, cake making or growing vegetables. On numerous occasions gifts of homemade edible goods, including delicious freshly laid eggs, have been exchanged, as a thanks and celebration of the collaborative process. Who knows what the common bond is, but for me, both influence my life in generous measures and both offer inspiration, discussion and hope.

If you are interested in purchasing the original limited edition book, please visit www.marydalton.co.uk. 10% of all sales go toward The Big Issue Foundation, registered charity number 1049077.

Embracing the Surplus and the Unwanted

Mary Dalton graduated from the Royal College of Art in 2008 with an MFA in Printmaking. Since then she has continued to work as an artist and collaborative printmaker in studios across the country. Most recently, she was senior studio printmaker at the world famous Curwen Print Studio. She has widely exhibited her work and continues to push the boundaries across many print media.

"Mary Dalton is an exceptional artist who excels at making things. This is the fundamental core of her passion for creating art…Her creativity is one we can care for, enjoy and interact with." Megan Fishpoole RE, 2012

Embracing the Surplus and the Unwanted

By Mary Dalton

For Andrew Street

Embracing the Surplus and the Unwanted

ood is about sharing. It is about using no more than we need; giving and using what we have in abundance; and celebrating all that we see as unwanted. As humans, understanding that food is essential for all should bring us closer together, not divide us. We should celebrate its common language and make the most of what we have, wasting little and giving more. Food is a necessity, but if we manage it more efficiently and if we share and learn from each other, then surely in the long term it will benefit everyone.

Basically we need to have an awareness of the value of our food. It is not about complex meals and flavours, but about understanding what we have and how we can use it effectively. Preventing food waste and giving up more time towards learning and understanding how to be more resourceful with food is not difficult. It really isn't. We do not need to dismiss good memories and fine flavours, but just be aware of what we have and what we can give. If we do not at least try, then can we claim to have any empathy towards those with whom food really is a matter of survival? If we have no empathy, can we call ourselves human? I couldn't. But perhaps I am a dreamer.

As well as being resourceful with food, we need to empathise with it and understand how preparing and eating food itself has a message. It contains in its tastes and its processes both love and hate, greed and sacrifice. It reflects how we feel, how we sense, how we express ourselves. From the most basic of economy biscuits dipped in tea to a home-made loaf of bread, food should be more that just sustenance. Yes it is comfort; it is indulgence or starvation; it is nutrition, energy and calories; it is romance or anger, or both, it is lazy and manic, practical or extravagant, it is bloated stomachs, rib cages; obesity, cream cakes, salads, curries, pasta, waffles, bread. But it is also something beyond this. Through the giving of something that is essential to all life, upon that moment of transfer we also share part of the passion and emotions that make up our own lives. We share the memories contained within its ingredients and cooking, ones that are held close to our hearts and then passed on to others. It can evoke emotions deep rooted in our body that only a fragrance or a flavour or process can bring rushing back with uncontrollable force. We should use its tastes, techniques and versatility as a language to express things that cannot be uttered in words, to cook and bake for those who need to laugh or cry, for those who need to pause and stop worrying, for those who need not to run about cooking for others, for people who need airlifted bread to survive, for those who want to romance, for everyone who has the capability to feel thank you, even if it is not ever said. Actions surely speak louder than words and there is no greater action that the selfless gift of food.

The following book contains recipes and stories, highlighting the importance of understanding the value of food, emotionally and physically, and how we can be more resourceful with the production and collection of food in our own homes and beyond. It is about learning, sharing and under-standing. This is the initial step in writing, and I hope that more will follow, expanding upon the questions, stories and recipes.

Mary Dalton

My Mother's Jam Making

Jams, jellies and chutneys: embracing the surplus and the unwanted

am very fortunate that I grew up with my parents' allotment providing most of our meals. My mother has the wonderful skill of being able to look at an unpredictable mass of recently picked produce, and conjure up an exceptionally tasty and bold meal. This is a credit to her own culinary skills and, moreover, a reflection upon her understanding of vegetables.

My mother, being the main vegetable grower, seems to always grow far more than is needed. Instead of 5 tomato plants, I remember one year she grew 20 varieties. We were tomatoed-out. Home made ketchup and chutney followed by the jar full. The same applies to the strawberries and soft fruits. I remember receiving a phone call saying she had just picked 4 kg of raspberries and then picked another 4 kg that she gave to the receptionists at the vets when she took our cat Jimmy in for an injection.

The strongest memory I have of the allotment is based upon one such soft fruit, strawberries. Imagine a summer day. The sky is lazy blue and the humid English heat is uncomfortable, made sicklier by scented heavy droplets of lavender bushes that line the allotment paths. The air has the taste of hot hay and cow breath sitting heavily on the fallow field adjoining the back end of the vegetable patches. Sitting amongst the strawberry bushes, eating the fresh fruit dipped in cream and sugar, I can understand why this is the taste of legends. Every red gem encompasses the taste of a June day, and only a few are enough to make you intoxicated.

Inevitably, from strawberries, jam making follows. When my mother made jam, steam would be rising, everything seemed to be slightly sticky, jam jars were being washed and sterilised, sugar being watched to make sure it did not burn. The news of the jam is something I look forward to every year. Last year the strawberry jam burnt, but I still forced it down, this year it looked good; a few years ago a quince butter was made that I am still cutting my way through now; a very good batch of raspberry jam, perfect for Victoria sponges, was made last season. Throughout the whole making process, I think I managed to evolve my body to require spoonfuls of warm cooking jam at every stage. Even now, as soon as I see a pot of jam, I have to go in with a spoon and eat a mound. The heavy intoxicating drug of its sweet, sickly memory is addictive in not always a responsible manner.

Surrounding the romanticism of jam making, there is a very important reason why it is in this book. Since my mother made pots and pots of jam, she would always have spare to give away. In fact I secretly believe that she makes more than is necessary in order to give it away. Nothing was wasted and all was shared. This resourcefulness and sharing extended to embrace others who had the raw fruit to give…

One such example is that of Damson jam. An elderly gentleman called Nelson Masters lived in one of the oldest houses in the village I was brought up in. In his garden was a wonderful Damson tree. The variety, called the Langley Bullace, is very localised to the area and was first introduced in 1902. Nelson's tree had such a wide girth that it would not surprise me if his was nearing that date in birth. Every year, it was laden with fruit and we were always invited over to strip the tree bare and make jam. I remember as a child being slightly scared of Nelson as he sat on his patio with a blanket over his knees and a walking stick. I also felt that the atmosphere was slightly sad because when we started making the Damson jam, Nelson was an elderly and frail man. So despite his obvious pleasure in seeing us all enjoy his fruit tree, every year the garden degraded around us, and in his final years Nelson never came to sit on the patio. This made it a mixture of pleasure and sadness.

Upon Nelson's death, the house was re-occupied by someone I was currently being employed by. On passing I mentioned the Damson tree and jam to Tina and she invited my mother and I back to pick more Damsons. We did so, and after the jam had set, we left her 4 pots of jam on her doorstep. Tina came back to me the following week with a wild wave of her hands and clothes and thanked my mother profusely for the best jam she had tasted. Whenever I see damsons, I think of Nelson and his jam and the pleasure it has given to many people. All for minimal cost and time, the sharing of jam and memories has made people smile with sadness and glee. And that is why jam is in this book.

The now famed Damson jam is stiff, with occasional gooey skins suspended in its dark black syrup. For me, it is a jam that tastes more of a fine red wine than a preserve. Its flavour is deep and soothing, to be savoured and swished around the mouth and left to coat the throat. It really is something special. Nelson of course was always given some pots as a thank you for allowing us to raid his magical tree. I always suspected they did not last long.

Surrounding the romanticism, and indeed mysticism, of the jam-brewing process, there is something about the vast quantities of jam my mum produced that represent what should be at the heart of good food. Sharing. The gift of home-made jam is one that represents the whole aspect of food, from the love of growing the fruit and the all-encompassing process of concocting, to the labelling of the pot and the giving of it to someone else.

MY MOTHER'S STRAWBERRY JAM

Makes: 3 x 200ml jars

INGREDIENTS:

450g strawberries (not over ripe or their will be problems setting.)

450g granulated sugar, or jam sugar with added pectin to aid setting

juice and grated rind of 1 lemon to each 450g of fruit to help setting

knob of unsalted butter

METHOD:

1. Prepare the fruit the day before. Mix the sugar with the fruit and leave. This allows the juices to run out. Do not put all the juice in, only half, as this will prevent the jam being too runny or boiling over.
2. Preheat the oven to 170°C, gas mark 3. To sterilise the jars, wash and rinse them and place them upside down on an oven rack and in the oven for 10 minutes or until thoroughly dry.
3. Increase the heat and bring to a vigorous boil for 5-10 minutes. Add the finely grated rind and juice of the lemon.
4. Add the butter to prevent scum forming. The boiling can vary slightly depending on the quantity

of fruit, and it is best to just test the jam as you go following the instructions below.

5. Remove from the heat and test the jam by dabbing a little on a cold plate. Cool for a minute in the fridge then push the jam with your fingertip. If it wrinkles, it has reached setting point. If not, boil for a further 2 minutes then test again. When the setting point is reached, let the jam cool for 20 minutes to prevent the fruit rising to the top once jarred. Spoon the jam into the hot jars and seal with the lids.

NELSON'S LANGLEY BULLACE JAM

Follow the weights and recipe above. Do not skin the bullace. There is no need to de-pip the bullace fruit, as when the jam is boiling, the stones will float to the top and you can skim them off.

FIG AND GINGER JAM

Follow the recipe above, using chopped ripe figs as the fruit. Slightly under-ripe figs may be used, especially if they are fresh from the tree! Add about 20g of freshly grated ginger or to taste.

GREENGAGE JAM WITH ZING

This recipe is the first of many donated by a wonderful cook and printmaker, Megan Fishpoole. I first had this delicious jam with a slice of her freshly baked bread, and we both had to have seconds, followed closely by thirds.

Makes: 4 x 200ml jars

INGREDIENTS:

450g greengages

6 apples

225g sugar

170g molasses [blackstrap if you want bitter tang]

or

170g maple syrup [if you want sweet woody tang]

METHOD:

1. Sterilize the jars and lids.
2. Peel, core and roughly chop the apples.
3. Place the apples in a pan with 4tbsp of water and gently heat until they are soft and mushy.
4. Place the greengages, sugar, syrup and apples into a pan.
5. Boil gently on a medium heat to reduce mixture for an hour and a half.
6. Test setting.
7. Jar.

ELDERFLOWER JELLY

Makes: 3-4 x 200ml jars

INGREDIENTS:

30 heads of fresh elderflowers (it is essential to use them as soon as they are picked)

1kg of apples

1kg of castor sugar

1 lemon

jelly bag, a pair of old tights or cheesecloth.

METHOD:

1. Sterilise the jars and lids.
2. Roughly chop the apples. No need to peel or core.
3. Place them in a large pan with the elderflower heads and enough water to cover the apples.
4. Bring to a boil and simmer for 30mins.
5. Place the contents into the jelly bag or cloth and leave to drain into a bowl overnight.
6. Measure the liquid and for every 600ml, place with 450g of castor sugar in a pan.
7. Bring to the boil slowly, stirring to dissolve the sugar. Boil rapidly for 10 minutes and then follow the setting test as for the strawberry jam.
8. If not setting, then squeeze the lemon juice in and keep trying! Bottle.

PINEAPPLE GERANIUM LEAF OR LEMON VERBENA JELLY

Following the recipe above, replace the elderflower heads with 20 crushed and torn pineapple geranium leaves.

WILD ROSE JELLY

Following the recipe above, replace the elderflower heads with a cup full of fresh wild rose (dog rose) petals. Once strained and setting point is reached, stir in a further half a cup full of fresh whole rose petal.

Utilising The Space We Have

The Mile End Garden: for The Twins, Mat and Cas, Tim and Tara

For those who do have access to an outdoor space, however small or concrete, then if you wish to, vegetables and fruit can still be grown. It really is quite incredible to amount that can be produced from the smallest of plots. My fiancé once lived in Mile End, in the heart of the East End, and his outdoor space consisted of a tiny concreted over patio. With the endorsement of The Twins who reside in the house, we attempted to grow our first vegetables. The experimental growing area consisted of 1 tonne of soil divided between two 1-cubic meter builders' sacks. This provided us with a raised bed of sorts. With the help of Tim, and Tara the Van, we collected 1 tonne of soil from a nursery of the M4, drove it back to London in the back of Tara's now sagging back, and then preceded to shovel it in bags from the front door, through the house, to the back patio. We had no wheelbarrow. The whole day was exhausting, but worth it. We had soil. Despite some technical difficulties along the way, the bags contained very healthy rows of kale, beetroot, carrots, leeks, turnips, ruby chard and lettuce. Our potatoes were in a jungle in the corner, planted out in refuse sacks containing our own compost. Giant garden spiders turned the tangle of leaves into their sanctuary. The following year we filled a third sack with our own beautiful, rich compost. This was the food for onions and garlic, important ingredients for everyone in the house.

The transformation of the patio in the East led us to meet the neighbours over the wall. The house is in a row of terraces, and many have low walls that allow us to talk to neighbours all around. Matt and Cas were very interested in out vegetable growing and though a number of friendly talks over the wall, we were allowed to climb over into their garden and turn the back end into an edible forest garden. This area of the garden was basically the builders' rubble dump with a small redundant pond, which Matt had filled with soil and compost. It is amazing how resilient fruit and vegetables are. It puts humans to shame. Our first plants in were a selection of herbs gathered as cuttings from my mum's garden, as well as a few small primrose plants with the hope they would take off and provide good ground cover and flowers in the spring and summer. The herbs rooted within a few weeks, and we all had a healthy supply of chives, marjoram, thyme, mint and fennel. We also planted two courgette plants, several broccoli seedlings, ruby chards, a jungle of parsley and three yellow raspberry canes. All of these have survived and thrived. Matt even built a little set of wooden steps straddling the wall so that we had ease of access between the gardens. It really is quite phenomenal the amount and the variance that can be produced from a small space. The following recipes are all invented taking inspiration from the produce we managed to grow in a patch of previously unused land.

MAT AND CAS'S SEPTEMBER GARDEN CHUTNEY

This is a very tasty chutney with a chunky texture. It is made with everything we had in the garden. Using fresh turmeric makes a big difference, both in colour and taste, but if it proves difficult to get hold of, replacing with the dried variety is perfectly acceptable.

INGREDIENTS:

1kg runner beans
3 onions
1 fennel bulb, finely chopped
2 large apples (cored, but not peeled)
2 pears (cored, but not peeled)
200g green tomatoes
8 sprays of elderberries
5 nasturtium seeds
1 chilli pepper (red)
5 garlic leaves
handful of chives
2tsp freshly grated turmeric or 3tsp dried turmeric powder.
2tsp cayenne pepper
salt and pepper
2 ½ tbsp cornflour
1kg sugar
1300ml malt vinegar

METHOD:

1. Top and tail the runner beans, and either shred or chop into small slices.
2. Finely chop the onions.
3. Add the beans and onions to boiling water, bring back to the boil and boil for 10 mins, or until the beans are just-tender. Drain.
4. Whilst the beans are boiling, finely chop the fennel, apple, pears and tomatoes.
5. Remove the elderberries from the sprays. Crush and finely chop the nasturtium seeds with the chilli, garlic leaves and chives.
6. Place the vinegar and sugar in a large pan, and slowly bring up to the boil, stirring to dissolve the sugar.
7. Once at the boil, add the beans, onions and fennel and simmer lightly for 15 mins.
8. Then add the pears, apples, tomatoes, elderberries, nasturtium seeds, chilli and garlic leaves along with the turmeric, cayenne and cornflour. Simmer for a further 15 mins.
9. Remove from the heat, leave to cool slightly and then pot into the hot jam jars.
10. Leave for a minimum of 3 months before eating (if you can!)

YOUNG BEETROOT GNOCCHI WITH CORIANDER AND LIME DRESSING

This was made with some very lovely young beetroot from the garden sacks. It really helps if you can get the smaller beetroot, similar in size to a golf ball, as they are sweeter and more tender.

Serves 3-4

INGREDIENTS:

275g potatoes
125g plain flour
1 egg, beaten
100g beetroot
salt and pepper

4tbsp olive oil
1 tbsp malt vinegar
1 green chilli
big bunch of fresh coriander
zest and juice of 1 lime
couple of drops of a very hot chilli sauce

METHOD:

1. Peel and scrub the potatoes and boil for 20-25mins or until tender. Drain.
2. Boil the beetroot whole for about 40mins, or until tender. Drain and rub the skins off. Leave to cool.
3. Place the potatoes and beetroot into a bowl. Smash together until smooth. Leave to cool.
4. Once cold, sieve the flour into the mix and add the beaten egg. Mix up until a dough forms. More flour or liquid may be added to get the desired stiff dough. Season to taste.
5. On a floured surface, roll out the dough to sausages about 1.5cm thick, then cut into length of about 3cm. Using a fork with the prongs upturned, press lightly into each gnocchi to create ridges. Once done, place the gnocchi onto a well floured surface and leave in the fridge whilst the dressing is being made.
6. For the dressing, finely chop the chilli (seeds optional depending on taste) and roughly chop the coriander leaves and finely chop the stalks.
7. Mix together with the oil, vinegar and lime.
8. To cook the gnocchi, bring a pan of water to the boil, and drop the gnocchi in. When they float to the surface, they are cooked. Drain.
9. Serve the gnocchi piping hot with the sauce drizzled over the top.

POTATO AND CHARD LEAF SALAD

This was made with the abundance of young chard and beet leaves we grew. Beetroot leaves are a very delicious addition to any salad or dish, and they also turn the meal a wonderful pink. This potato dish goes maroon. It is quite stunning.

Serves 3-4

INGREDIENTS:

600g potatoes
a big handful of chard or beet leaves, including stalks
1 clove of garlic
a handful of chives
couple of stalks of thyme
salt and pepper to taste
4tbsp olive oil
1tbsp balsamic vinegar
2tbsp crème fraiche or soured cream

METHOD:

1. Finely chop the stalks of the chard, and loosely shred the leaves.
2. Crush the garlic and finely chop the herbs.
3. Scrub, but do not peel, the potatoes and chop them into big chunks.
4. Place in a pan of boiling water and simmer until tender.

5. 2 minutes before the potatoes are ready, place the chard stalks into the boiling water. Drain.
6. Place the cooked potatoes and stalks into a bowl and mix with the oil and vinegar. It is essential the potatoes are still warm as this allows them to absorb the oil.
7. Mix through the chard leaves, the garlic, seasoning and crème fraiche.
8. Serve warm.

BROCCOLI, APPLE AND BROAD BEAN DIP

Serves 5-6 with bread

INGREDIENTS:

300g broccoli
100g podded broad beans
100g hard cheese, preferably parmesan
1 apple, cored and roughly chopped.
1 onion
2 green chillis
1 clove of garlic
1 tsp cumin powder
dash of Worcester sauce
salt and pepper
olive oil

METHOD:

1. Break the broccoli into florets and chop the stalk. Boil for about 10 minutes, or until tender.
2. Boil the broad beans for about 5 minutes.
3. Finely chop the onion, garlic and chilli. Fry gently for 10 mins with the cumin powder. Add the chopped apple. Fry for a further 5 mins.
4. Place the onion mixture with the broccoli and beans into a food processor and blitz until smooth, but still slightly grainy. Stir through the seasoning and Worcester sauce to taste.

GATHERING FROM AROUND US: PARASOLS AND OYSTERS

rowing your own produce is essential if you are able. But even without the space, wild food is around us in abundance to pick and utilise. Mushrooms are one of my passions. But, as always, never ever eat a mushroom unless you are 100% certain of what it is. Even then ere on the side of caution if in any doubt.

The best time to hunt mushrooms is early in the morning. I have never known whether this is because other mushroom hunters might pick the mushrooms before you, or because the woodland always looks more beautiful in the morning, or that if you find a big hoard they are good cooked down with butter and garlic and slathered on toast for you lunch. I like to think it is the later, although the middle one is also a very good option. I can't quite believe that there are groups of dawn mushroom hunters elbowing each other out of the way in forests to get to the best Cep for their lunch. Although it is a wondrous image non-the-less. However, I still like to go early in the morning because it is such a pleasure and privilege to be able to walk through an oak forest as the sun stretches its wings, knowing that some of the trees you brush past are actually up to five-hundred years old, seeing more in their lifetimes than I can even remember learning from my history lessons. That alone is enough of a reason to drag yourself out of bed on a cold dreggy morning and to pull on rubber boots.

The greater pleasure comes when you find your first mushroom. Parasols are one of the commonest varieties and are also very easy to spot, looking like a squat umbrella shading the grass beneath from Autumnal rains. But for me, one of the most precious and beautiful of mushrooms to find is the oyster mushroom. It is still relatively common, although when you see a cluster of oysters gripping onto a branch, all commonality is replaced by sheer awe. Wild oyster mushrooms look nothing like their insipid counterpart found plasticized in supermarkets. I've picked oysters up to 15cm in diameter and of a pearl pink colour so soft it feels like cold hand cream on dry hands. Their perfume is delicate; more a flavour than a scent and it lingers and caresses your hands rather than over-powering your senses.

The cauliflower fungus is a very bizarre object. It grows on the roots of woodland trees, I think my parents discovered theirs on a beech tree, and it looks, as it names suggests, like a cauliflower foraging in the woodland scrub. The specimen we found had to be carried home in the hood of one of our coats as it was too big for the bag. Once it was inspected, we decided the best method to treat it was to dry out small slivers and keep them for using as dried mushrooms to add extra deep flavour to dishes. The slivers got placed in a jam jar, with the Latin name, Sparassis Crispa, on the front. They look like wood shavings picked up from a joiner's floor and preserved as an anatomical specimen. The scent when the lid is opened is one that is knitted, felted, woollen and most definitely with a hint of dark chocolate with a handful of fresh nuts cooked through. Undeniably delicious.

MUSHROOMS ON TOAST

Simple, but if done correctly, so yummy and good.

Serves 1

INGREDIENTS:

A very large handful of mushrooms
A large handful of fresh parsley, roughly chopped
1 clove of garlic finely chopped
Pepper
20g butter
olive oil

METHOD:

1. Brush the mushrooms to remove any dirt, but do not wash as they will absorb the water and go soggy.
2. Gently tear the mushrooms up into chunks. Tearing fresh mushrooms is better as it will not damage them as mush as cutting.
3. Heat the butter and a dash of olive oil in a pan until hot, and add the mushrooms.
4. Stirring regularly, cook the mushrooms on a medium heat until the first of their juices are released.
5. Then immediately add the garlic and parsley, stir through for 20 seconds and take of the heat and serve on warm toast.

PARASOL AND OYSTER MUSHROOM RISOTTO

Serves 2-4

INGREDIENTS:
300g risotto rice
1 small onion
2 cloves of garlic
5 parasol heads
large handful of oyster mushrooms
A couple of sprigs of marjoram
50g butter
100g grated parmesan
2 litres of water
Vegetable stock
Olive oil
Seasoning

METHOD:

1. Brush the mushrooms of any dirt. Do not wash them, they absorb the water and become soggy. Roughly tear up both the parasol and the oysters.
2. Finely chop the onion and fry slowly and gently in olive oil.
3. Bring the water to the boil and add the stock.
4. Add half the marjoram and mushrooms and fry for 5 minutes, stirring frequently.

5. Turn onto a low heat. Add the rice and stir gently until the rice is coated and transparent at the edges.
6. Add the first ladle of stock and stir.
7. When the water has all evaporated, add the next ladle and gently stir. Continue in this manner until the risotto is soft, the rice cooked through, but still with a bite, and the majority of the stock all used. It should take about 30-40 minutes.
8. Once done, take off the heat and sprinkle with the parmesan, remaining marjoram and the dabs of butter. Place the lid on and leave for 5 minutes before stirring. Serve up piping hot.

Fresh, Wild Foods: Nature's Surplus

unting for wild foods is a real pleasure in the UK, since we have such varied and abundant countryside; the wild foods on offer are equally as rich. Using what is available around us is so valuable in understanding the abundance of nature and also a vital lesson in how to make the most of what is bestowed upon us. Foraging accustoms us to our seasons, to what is available throughout the year and how we may use it in inventive and sustainable ways. Wild samphire and sea beet emanate the flavours of the sea like no other ingredient, and young wild garlic seeps a milky taste nothing like the dried bulb variety. Of course, when picking wild foods, respect has to be shown to the plant and the natural setting. Imagine that you are picking only what is surplus from nature - bushes should never be stripped, always leaving fruit and berries for birds and wildlife, and plants should never be pulled up. If we show respect to nature, then it will remain bountiful and abundant for many more generations.

Hazelnuts are one of my favourites foods to gather. Firstly, they are very simple to know when they are ready to pick, as they fall quite readily on the floor. Secondly, it is highly satisfying to run your hands through a big bagful of nuts. It is a combination of toes running through wet sand and the clicking together empty coconut shells. However, the pleasures of picking are sometimes outweighed by the mammoth task of shelling the little nuts. I've found the best way is to hit them on the top (non-pointy end) with a metal headed hammer onto a block of hard wood. This works well without crushing the nut. This year, we collected 3.6kg of hazelnuts. And they are absolutely delicious. Their soft, milky, sweet texture is nothing like the dried, dusty blobs in health food stores. It may take longer, but as with all foods harvested by your own hands, the time invested pays off with the same abundance in which nature gave her fruits.

A neighbour once told me that she had found some wild raspberries, and if this was the case, then a celebration is needed for it would be the first time I would have come across wild raspberries in an urban setting. Even if she mistook them for under-ripe blackberries, that is still worth jumping for, because the blackberry bush is one of the most generous fruits around. Every year the plant flowers and fruits happily even in the most unforgiving of places. The happy berries existence is like a sign to believe in life, no matter how tough sometimes it may feel. Its juicy produce can be used to make cordials, jams, desserts, jellies or just eaten on its own with some cold cream. It truly is a wonderfully giving plant, and every year it amazes me to see people buying packaged vacumised blackberries from the supermarket. Through generations of these plastic fruits, we have lost our sense of the season and the treats each supply. Which is sad, but there is also hope as many people return to responsibly picking them from the hedgerow. I particularly like to make blackberry cake, which is a version of a Victoria sponge with blackberry syrup in the mix and in the butter-cream, with blackberries in the middle and on top. The cake turns a light purple, the butter icing candy pink and the blackberries remain glossy black. With the sugary syrup in the cake mix, the resulting sponge has a texture of silk, and the juices from the fresh blackberries scattered around leek and soak into the sponge, making it more of a dessert than a cake.

The following recipes are all deserts and mainly wild food cakes. Why cakes? Well, why not. Cakes are good. Each one uses ingredients that have all been picked wild, and picked with a love of what nature provides for free. I want to thank Traditional London Sponge Cake, the specialists in wonderful wild and free cakes, for donating the stunning cake recipes.

WILD STRAWBERRY AND CHERRY CRUMBLE

Wild strawberries do grow in the UK, if you are prepared to share them with the blackbirds! They grow very well on the continent, particularly in more Southern climes. I remember picking lots of little strawberries as a child in a wooded glen in France. They were like gems of magic. If you do not find enough strawberries, then just replace them with the cherries.

Serves 4

INGREDIENTS:

200g wild strawberries
250g wild cherries, stoned
1tbsp castor sugar

crumble:

200g plain flour
25g fine semolina
110g soft butter or margarine
75g castor sugar

22cm diameter baking dish, or similar, approximately 4cm deep.

METHOD:

1. 1. Pre heat the oven to 180°c/350°F/gas mark 4 and grease the baking dish.

2. Roughly chop the strawberries and cherries and place in the dish and sprinkle with the 1tbsp sugar.
3. Place the crumble ingredients in a bowl and rub together with your fingertips until the texture of breadcrumbs is reached.
4. Mix in 2 tbsp of cold water to form a few clumps.
5. Sprinkle the crumble over the fruit and splash with cold water.
6. Bake for 30 minutes or until slightly golden on top.

APPLE, PEAR AND HAZELNUT CRUMBLE

INGREDIENTS:
250g wild apples
200g wild pears
2tbsp brown sugar

Crumble:
200g plain flour
25g fine semolina
75g fresh hazelnuts, crushed
110g soft butter or margarine
75g brown castor sugar

22cm diameter baking dish, approximately 5cm deep.

METHOD:

1. Pre heat the oven to 180°c/350°F/gas mark 4 and grease the baking dish.
2. Roughly chop the apples and pears and place in the dish and sprinkle with the 2tbsp sugar.
3. Place the crumble ingredients in a bowl and rub together with your fingertips until the texture of breadcrumbs is reached.
4. Sprinkle the crumble over the fruit and splash with cold water.
5. Bake for 30 minutes or until slightly golden on top.

WILD CORDIALS

This base recipe can be used with any wild fruit or leaf that you fancy. Try water mint leaves, elderberries or blackberries. All are very refreshing served with ice.

INGREDIENTS:

1 kg sugar
500ml water
150g of the wild ingredient
old cleaned milk containers, or similar plastic/glass drinks bottles
jelly strainer or fine cloth

METHOD:

1. Place the sugar and water in a pan and slowly heat until the sugar dissolves.
2. Add the wild ingredient.
3. Bring to the boil and simmer for 10 minutes and then take off the heat. Leave to sit with a lid on for 24 hours.
4. Strain through a jelly strainer or cloth and bottle.
5. Store in the fridge. Dilute about 1 portion of syrup to 4 water, or to taste.

ELDERBERRY SYRUP

This is a very unusual recipe to make a sweet syrup. It is very tasty drizzled over porridge, but equally delicious as a marinade for pork or used in sweet savoury asian cooking. It is thick like molasses, and purple like a king's velvet cape.

Makes 2-3 jam jars

INGREDIENTS:

400g of elderberries
800g castor sugar
jelly strainer, pair of clean old tights or a large piece of cheesecloth/muslin

METHOD:

1. Sterilise the jars and lids.
2. Place the elderberries and sugar in a pan and squash the berries until juices are released.
3. Heat on a low setting until the sugar dissolves, stirring continuously.
4. Bring to a boil and boil rapidly for 10 minutes.
5. Strain through a jelly strainer of cloth, collecting the juice.
6. Leave the juice to cool and bottle.

BLACKBERRY CAKE

INGREDIENTS:

175g self raising flour
175g castor sugar
175g soft butter
3 eggs

80g icing sugar
35g soft butter

50g fresh blackberries
20g castor sugar

2 tbsp blackberry jam

METHOD:

1. Pre heat the oven to 180°c/350°F/gas mark 4 and grease and line the base of two 20cm/8" sandwich cake tins.
2. Place the blackberries in a pan with a tablespoon of water and the 20g of castor sugar. Bring to the simmer on a low heat, dissolving the sugar. Simmer for 5 minutes and leave to cool completely. Do not drain.
3. Cream the butter and the sugar until pale and very soft.
4. Whisk in the eggs, one at a time.

5. Sieve in the flour to the mix and 2 tablespoons of the blackberry juice from step 2. Fold in well.
6. Split the mixture between the two tins and bake for 20-25 minutes until a knife comes out of the centre cleanly. Turn out and leave to cool on a wire rack.
7. Make the butter-cream by sieving the icing sugar into a bowl and creaming it gently with the butter. Once mixed, add 1 tbsp of the blackberry juice and mix well.
8. Spread the jam, butter cream and half the blackberries between the two cakes, and sandwich together.
9. Finally, sprinkle the remaining blackberries on top of the cake, and drizzle any remaining juice evenly over. Sprinkle with icing sugar.

WILD FIG AND RICOTTA CAKE

This is another wonderful pudding cake, and particularly good served with cream. It is inspired by a wild fig tree we found in the Italian town of Lucca, which provided us with a bag full of warm, indulgent Italian figs.

INGREDIENTS:

175g self raising flour
175g castor sugar
175g soft butter
3 eggs
1 tbsp milk
200g ricotta

100g of freshly picked soft figs
2 tbsp of runny honey

METHOD:

1. Pre heat the oven to 180°c/350°F/gas mark 4 and grease and line the base of two 20cm/8" sandwich cake tins.
2. Roughly chop half the figs and place in a pan with the honey and 1 tbsp of water. Bring to the boil and simmer for 10 minutes. Leave to cool completely. Do not drain.
3. Cream the butter and the sugar until pale and very soft.
4. Whisk in the eggs, one at a time.

5. Sieve in the flour to the mix and add half of the cooked figs, but not the juice. Fold in well. Add the milk and fold.
6. Split the mixture between the two tins and bake for 20-25 minutes until a knife comes out of the centre cleanly. Turn out and leave to cool on a wire rack.
7. Spread ½ the ricotta onto one cake and then sprinkle over the remaining fig and honey mixture, leaving 1tbsp of the liquid behind. Place the second cake on top.
8. Finally, cut the remaining whole figs into quarters and place on the top of the cake and dollop the remaining ricotta between. Drizzle with the retained honey and fig juice. Sprinkle with icing sugar.

TOFFEE APPLE CAKE

This cake is very sweet and a wonderful way to welcome in the Autumn months with her bonfires and glowing leaves.

INGREDIENTS:

175g self raising flour

175g castor sugar

175g soft butter

3 eggs

80g icing sugar

35g soft butter

2 wild apples, cored and chopped into small chunks

75g butter

75g brown sugar

100ml double cream

2 tbsp crab apple jelly, or similar

METHOD:

1. Pre heat the oven to 180°c/350°F/gas mark 4 and grease and line the base of two 20cm/8" sandwich cake tins.
2. Start by making the toffee sauce. Gently melt the butter and dissolve in the sugar.
3. Once the sugar has dissolved, slowly mix in the cream. Bring to a simmer, and rapidly simmer for 5 minutes, until it turns caramel coloured. Leave to cool.

4. Cream the butter and the sugar until pale and very soft.
5. Whisk in the eggs, one at a time.
6. Sieve in the flour to the mix, add the apples and 3tbsp of the toffee sauce from step 4. Fold in gently until well mixed.
7. Split the mixture between the two tins and bake for 20-25 minutes until a knife comes out of the centre cleanly. Turn out and leave to cool on a wire rack.
8. Make the butter-cream with the addition of 1 tbsp of toffee sauce.
9. Spread a layer of crab apple jelly onto one cake, then the butter-cream, and finally place the second cake on top.

NETTLE MADEIRA LOAF

The leaves of the nettles must be picked young and in Springtime, otherwise they are slightly bitter. The sting will disappear on blanching. The nettles make this cake surprisingly savoury, with a wonderful earthy overtone. Very tasty with sour cream.

INGREDIENTS:

225g self raising flour
50g fine semolina
175g castor sugar
175 soft butter
3 eggs
about 30 fresh spring nettle leaves

METHOD:

1. Pre-heat the oven to 150°C/300°F/gas mark 2. Grease and line the base of a 900g loaf tin.
2. Blanch the nettle leaves for 2 minutes and drain. Chop until a pulp is formed.
3. Cream together the butter and sugar until pale.
4. Whisk in the eggs, one at a time.
5. Sieve in the flour and semolina and add the pulp. Fold everything together gently until mixed.
6. Place into the prepared tin and bake for 1 – 11/4 hours, or until a knife comes out clean.

FENNEL SEED LOAF

A really wonderful cake tasting exactly the same as red aniseed balls. Wild fennel can often be found of waste-land where you can collect a whole year's supply from its generous web like heads.

INGREDIENTS:

225g self raising flour
50g fine semolina
175g castor sugar
175 soft butter
3 eggs
1 tbsp fresh fennel seeds

85g icing sugar
35g butter
2tsp milk

METHOD:

1. Pre-heat the oven to 150°C/300°F/gas mark 2. Grease and line the base of a 900g loaf tin.
2. Crush the fennel seeds.
3. Cream together the butter and sugar until pale.
4. Whisk in the eggs, one at a time.
5. Sieve in the flour and semolina and add two thirds of the fennel seeds. Fold everything together gently until mixed.

6. Place into the prepared tin and bake for 1 – 11/4 hours, or until a knife comes out clean. Leave to cool
7. Cream the icing sugar and butter together with milk.
8. Mix in the remaining fennel seeds and spread on the top of the loaf.

Celebrating the Unwanted

athering wild foods stems from not wanting to see things go to waste. Those who gather not only experience the pleasure in picking and eating the freshest produce, but we also like to see things used. This also means using ingredients that many see as unusable. In the market I worked at, food would be regularly thrown away in the skips. At the end of each day, a select group would gather and pick out what fruit and vegetables they could find. The majority of the produce was perfectly edible. I have picked out many vegetables and used them, and it is far better to do that then see them go to waste and mould. On one occasion, we picked out about 10kg of French beans. We went through them to throw away the few mouldy ones, and the rest went into one of the best chutneys I think I have tasted! On another occasion, an Italian lady and myself shared a crate full of stunning Chanterelle mushrooms. They went straight onto toast with garlic and butter. On one occasion, I ended up with a handful of some of the largest and most thick-skinned lemons I had ever seen for free. I never know what to really do with lemons, so I made two very different, but beautifully flavoursome risottos, and used the rest to make a batch of preserved lemons. If you do not want to waste even the smallest amount of food, then your mind has to become quite agile in order to use up the ingredient. This is both fun and inventive.

I am a big fan of pastry, and home-made pastry really is not difficult. Pies are also a wonderful way to use up any odds and ends that you may have in the kitchen. I am a staunch believer in onion tart, as it is the perfect way to use up the last onions before they go off. I have included a recipe for Meg's American Pie Crust, which is absolutely delicious, and two wonderful fillings, pumpkin and egg custard. Pumpkins always come in abundance during Autumn and it is always a sad waste to scoop out the innards for lanterns and then throw it away. Try Meg's recipe, it is a classic and beautiful pie.

Part of the prevention of food waste is using everything that we can, however odd it may seem. A friend of mine was walking his dog in the New Forest, when he came across the warm carcass of a female red deer. He suspected a car had killed her. She had evidently fell recently and not a bone had been broken. Here is an interesting conundrum. Do you leave her to rest as she fell, providing the woodland animals with food and the forest floor with nutrients? Or do you not waste the food that her meat may provide for you and many others? Surely if the animal is respected and treated well, then using the deer as a source of meat is not wrong? However we also do not understand enough about animals to presume that a dead doe is not mourned by her stag, or that her meat will not feed and sustain the local forest animals. I do not know what I would do, but I certainly do not hold it against those who would choose to use her meat. It is a really tough one. Mike chose to carefully carry the carcass back to his car and he hung it up to bleed. He took her to his local butcher, who was willing to butcher the deer for free in exchange for half the meat. He then generously gave us a whole haunch of the stunning red venison. We took the meat, as we were grateful for such a wondrous treat. I have never cut such wonderfully tender and deep purple meat as that leg. I hope we honoured the life of the doe by treating and cooking her meat with love and respect. And though my mind is still split as to what to do in such a situation, I would rather eat that deer than any commercially bred and slaughtered animal, who will not be treated with nearly as much as the respect it deserves.

FRENCH BEAN AND FRESH TURMERIC CHUTNEY

Makes approx 6-8 jars. Sterilize the jars and lids.

INGREDIENTS:

1kg French beans
4-5 onions
20g fresh turmeric, peeled
700g Demerara sugar
900ml malt vinegar
1tbsp cayenne pepper
2 tsp paprika
1 tsp mustard powder
1tsp freshly ground coriander seed
1 ½ tbsp cornflour

METHOD:

1. Top and tail the French beans, and slice into 2cm lengths. Finely chop the onions.
2. Place the onions and beans into a pan of boiling water and boil for 8 mins. Drain.
3. Place the sugar and vinegar into a large pan and heat slowly to dissolve the sugar.
4. Once dissolved, add the beans, onions, spices, cornflour and grate in all the turmeric.
5. Bring to the boil and boil for 15 minutes or until thickened.
6. Allow to cool for 20 minutes, stir, and bottle.

MEG'S SWEET GARDEN CHUTNEY

"I made the garden chutney up at the spur of the moment! Just all the fruit that was in the kitchen at the time." And that, Meg, is why it is so tasty and wonderful.

Makes: 3 x 200ml jars

INGREDIENTS:

1 onion, finely chopped
1 tomato, finely chopped
325g sugar
1tsp Worcestershire sauce
3 apples
6 pears
1 orange

METHOD:

1. Place the onion and tomato in a pan with 100g of the sugar and the Worcestershire sauce.
2. Gently and slowly heat, so that the sugar dissolves in the tomato juice and sauce.
3. Slowly keep the mixture simmering until the onion is caramalising. Stir frequently.
4. Steam the apples and pears until soft.
5. Place the fruit and onion mixture into a pan with the orange juice and the remaining 225g of sugar.
6. Bring to the boil and simmer for an hour and a half until sticky and chunky. Bottle.

LEMON AND TURMERIC RISOTTO

Serves 4 (with spare for patties the next day)

INGREDIENTS:

300g risotto rice

1 small onion, finely diced

Olive oil

About 50g of fresh turmeric root, peeled and finely grated

2 lemons

Small handful of fresh parsley, roughly chopped

50g butter

2 litres of water

Seasoning

METHOD:

1. Bring the water up to a simmer and maintain the simmer.
2. Thickly cut the rind off both lemons and chop finely and add to the simmering water to make a lemon stock.
3. Cut up the remaining flesh into rough chunks.
4. Fry the onion slowly in the olive oil until lightly golden and soft.
5. Add the rice and the chunks of lemon and stir around in the oil and onion until the rice appears slightly translucent at the edges.

6. Add the first ladle of stock and stir well.
7. Turn the heat right down and leave, stirring occasionally, until the stock has all been absorbed and it appears quite dry. Add the next ladle full of stock.
8. Repeat this process, stirring more and more, until enough stock has been added to allow the rice to go stick and soft. Testing is essential.
9. With the final ladle of stock, add all the grated turmeric.
10. Let the last of the stock become absorbed by the rice and then turn the heat off.
11. Break up the butter into small lumps and dot around the top of the risotto and leave covered for 5 minutes.
12. After 5 minutes, stir in the butter and the parsley and season to taste.

RADICCHIO AND LEMON RISOTTO

Serves 4

INGREDIENTS:

300g risotto rice
1 small onion, finely diced
2 garlic cloves, finely chopped
Olive oil
1 large head of radicchio, shredded
1 lemon
Small handful of fresh thyme
50g butter
2 litres of water
1 stock cube/1 heaped tsp vegetable stock (or just bung in some old veg into the water)
150g freshly grated parmesan
1 small chilli, finely chopped
Seasoning

METHOD:

1. Bring the water up to a simmer and maintain the simmer.
2. Finely dice the rind and the flesh of the lemon.
3. Fry the onion slowly in the olive oil until lightly golden and soft.
4. Add the garlic in at the end to prevent burning and to keep the flavour fresh.

5. Add the rice, the lemon rind and half the shredded radicchio and stir around in the oil and onion until the rice appears slightly translucent at the edges.
6. Add the first ladle of stock and stir well.
7. Turn the heat right down and leave, stirring occasionally, until the stock has all been absorbed and it appears quite dry. Add the next ladle full of stock.
8. Repeat this process, stirring more and more, until enough stock has been added to allow the rice to go stick and soft. Testing is essential.
9. With the final ladle of stock, add the lemon flesh and the remaining radicchio and stir well.
10. Let the last of the stock become absorbed by the rice and then turn the heat off.
11. Break up the butter into small lumps and dot around the top of the risotto and sprinkle all the parmesan on top and leave covered for 5 minutes.
12. After 5 minutes, stir the risotto and finally add the thyme leaves.
13. Delicious served with a basic green salad.

HOME MADE PLAIN AMERICAN PIE CRUST

makes one 9" single crust pie

INGREDIENTS:

200g cup plain flour

100g vegetable fat

½ tsp salt

4 to 5 tablespoons of cold water

METHOD:

1. Grease the dish well.
2. Mix the flour and salt together in a large bowl.
3. Cut in the fat using a fork until the size of small peas.
4. Sprinkle in 1tbsp of water and toss until mixed.
5. Continue mixing the water, a tbsp at a time.
6. Gather the dough into a ball.
7. Roll on a floured surface until a circle is formed big enough to line and overflow the dish.
8. Transfer the crust into the dish, allowing the edge to over-hang slightly.

MUM'S MUM, MY MUM'S, MINE NOW PUMPKIN PIE (MEG'S PUMPKIN PIE)

Makes enough for one 9" crust pie

INGREDIENTS:

575g of pumpkin, peeled, de-seeded and in chunks
130g sugar
1 tsp ground cinnamon
1 tsp ground ginger
1/4 tsp vanilla
2 large eggs
410g can of evaporated milk

METHOD:

1. Pre-heat the oven to 220°C/425°F/Gas Mark 7.
2. Steam the pumpkin soft, then mash to a puree.
3. Mix sugar, pinch of salt, cinnamon, ginger and vanilla in a bowl.
4. Beat eggs in a separate larger bowl. Add the pumpkin puree plus the sugar and spice mix.
5. Add the evaporated milk, slowly and stirring all the time.
6. Pour the mixture into the prepared crust pie.
7. Bake in the oven for 15 minutes, then lower the temperature to 175°C/350°C/gas mark 4 and bake for 45 minutes more.
8. Cool on a rack for 2 hours before serving.

MEG'S MUM'S BAKED CUSTARD

Makes enough for a 1 pint casserole dish. Or it may fill a 9" crust pie, follow the same recipe below without the roasting tin method.

INGREDIENTS:

3 beaten eggs
50g granulated sugar
480ml of milk
½ tsp salt
½ tsp of vanilla
½ tsp ground cinnamon
½ tsp freshly grated nutmeg

METHOD:

1. Pre heat the oven to 160°C/325°F/gas mark 3.
2. Begin by heating the milk up very quickly until boiling and then boil rapidly for 1 minute. Leave to cool.
3. Mix the eggs, sugar and salt.
4. Stir in the milk and vanilla essence.
5. Pour into the dish and place gently into a deep roasting pan and place in the oven.
6. Fill the roasting pan with water to a depth of 2cm.
7. Bake for 45 minutes.
8. Sprinkle with the cinnamon and nutmeg.

PLAINS INDIAN VENISON STEW

This is the recipe we used to cook the leg of venison given to us by Mike. It was stunning.

INGREDIENTS:

1.75kg venison cut into cubes
2 large yellow onions
4 strips of bacon
2L of water
6 juniper berries crushed
berries from 5 heads of elderberries
1tsp cayenne pepper
1tbsp elderberry syrup (see previous recipe) or molasses
1tbsp of cornflour
(optional) 5 ripe tomatoes washed quartered

METHOD:

1. Cut the onions finely, and chop the bacon into chunks.
2. Place all the ingredients into a large pan and bring to the boil.
3. Simmer uncovered for 3 hours.
4. After 3 hours, it should be thick and gravy like. If not, add 1tbsp of cornflour and simmer for 20 minutes more.

Bread

The Food For Sharing and Understanding

read. The final chapter and in many ways, the most simple. Bread is a staple across the world, and saves lives in many famine-ravished countries. It is something so simple and elemental, that I do not see any excuse why more people do not at least attempt to make their own bread. Not only is the taste completely different from the shop bought variety, but making your own bread gives this food the respect it deserves.

When you bake your first loaf, I would be surprised if you do not become completely addicted. It is the smell. It fills your home and your taste buds. The first five minutes in the oven are full of fresh yeast aromas, clingy and slightly nauseating, and then as the crust forms, it smells of sweet earth. Bread, of all foods, is there to be shared, and it can bring people together in ways that no other food can. From the kneading, the two risings, the addition of flavours, the baking, the slight cooling and finally the tearing of a hunk to eat with a dab of melting butter on top. If you make someone bread, you have probably won their heart. It certainly won mine. We should celebrate bread for all its life-giving properties and it wondrous taste. Making bread shows to the world that you are committed to celebrating and treasuring the most valuable of foods. Warm bread says what most people can't even speak. It is worth every second of effort and time.

I worked for a long period of time at a fantastic fruit and vegetable stall at a London's famous Borough Market. The week before I was due to leave, I got into a discussion about bread making with one of the regulars, a lovely man called Mark. He mentioned that he made his bread from his own yeast culture that was given to him by his friend Sam. The next week, my last day on the stall, Mark bumped into us grabbing our breakfast and whipped out of his bag a small kilner jar with about 1cm of what can only be described as off-white bubbly gunk in the bottom. He had brought us some of his yeast culture. The culture meant that not only did we never had to use unreliable commercial or dried yeast, but we could also grow the yeast culture in some of our own milled flour so that we could have a reliable yeast to work effectively with the high protean and gluten product we were milling. It was an incredible gift and one that we hope to pass on to others. Imagine that, one yeast culture will pass through generations and across families to help in the process of bread making. To me, that is a phenomenal thought.

Bread encapsulates everything that good food should be. It should be shared, it should be fresh, and we should always put time and effort into understanding, developing and preparing it. Food keeps us alive and also gives many people pleasure in taste, texture and smell. It should not be associated with greed, but with sharing. I can only thank you for reading this far, and I hope that it inspires you to go out there and pick the food around us, to try to learn and question about how we may reduce waste, and to perhaps, I can only ask, to try growing something of your own. It really is worth it for now and for the future. So to end, a bread recipe form someone who, over the last few years, has learnt and challenged his own understanding of food ten fold, and for this, someone I also learn from. The recipe is still evolving, and most certainly requires your own experimentation with the yeast and the flour to produce the most successful result. There is no harm in experimentation, accepting and learning from the failings and celebrating the successes. This keeps food energised. And it keeps us questioning and learning. With that, we can understand more about our food and how it can benefit us all.

ANDREW'S FRESH YEAST BREAD

Note, working with fresh yeast depends on many factors, and it is best to train your yeast culture with the flour you use.

This makes a large cob, or a 900g loaf.

INGREDIENTS:

600g string white bread flour
1tsp salt
2tbsp sugar
1tsp fresh yeast culture
450ml warm water

oven tray for a cob, 900g loaf tin for a loaf

METHOD:

1. Place half the warm water in a bowl and dissolve the yeast culture in it.
2. Mix the flour, salt and sugar in a bowl.
3. Mix in the yeast culture and water in the flour mixture. This will make a very wet dough. Do not be put off by this, it is good.
4. Knead for 5-10 minutes. Again, it will be sticky and wetter than most dough, but do persist,
5. Place in a large bowl and place a plastic carrier bag over the top.
6. Leave to rise in a warm place for anywhere between 12 and 18 hour, or until doubled in size.

7. Re-knead the dough for 2-5 minutes, adding any flavouring if desired.
8. For a cob, form a ball of dough and place on a floured oven tray, for a loaf place the dough in a floured bread tin.
9. Cover with plastic bag again, and leave in a warm place to rise for a couple of hours.
10. Pre-heat the oven to 200°C/400°F/gas mark 6.
11. When risen, place the bread in the oven and cook for 25-30 minutes, or until the bread sounds hollow when taped on the base. Andrew says do not be afraid to put the bread back in if unsure.
12. When done, sit back, break open, smile and enjoy. You made it.

FRESH YEAST STARTER

How to make your own natural, or wild, yeast starter used in the bread recipe above. It is important to use a glass bowl so that there will be no reaction with the mixture to effect the yeast development.

1. In a glass bowl mix 75g of bread flour with 120ml of water until smooth. Cover with a tea towel or cheesecloth and secure the sides and leave overnight.
2. In the morning add 2 tbsp of water and 2 tbsp of flour and mix. Cover. Mix again in the evening and cover.
3. Leave covered for 4-5 days, when it will start to show bubbles.
4. Leave for a further 2-3 days and then it may be used.
5. Keep about 3cm of the yeast starter in a sealed glass jar, such as a jam jar. If you are using it regularly, then it needs to be refreshed every day by removing all but 1 tsp of the starter and adding 2 tbsp of bread flour and 2 tbsp of water into the jar. Mix thoroughly.
6. If you are going away for a while or having a break from bread making, then the yeast starter can be stored in the fridge for a very long period. When ready to be used again, it will just need refreshing for a few days.

www.ingramcontent.com/pod-product-compliance
Ingram Content Group UK Ltd.
Pitfield, Milton Keynes, MK11 3LW, UK
UKHW020218250726
13967UKWH00001B/59
9 781300 693550